Watching
The River
Flow By:
Selected Poems

ROBERT TRABOLD, Ph.D

BALBOA.
PRESS
A DIVISION OF HAY HOUSE

Balboa Press books may be ordered through booksellers or by contacting:

Balboa Press
A Division of Hay House
1663 Liberty Drive
Bloomington, IN 47403
www.balboapress.com
1 (877) 407-4847

Print information available on the last page.

ISBN: 978-1-5043-6269-6 (sc)
ISBN: 978-1-5043-6271-9 (hc)
ISBN: 978-1-5043-6270-2 (e)

Library of Congress Control Number: 2016911972

Balboa Press rev. date: 08/03/2016

Acknowledgments

Soul Fountain, *Ravens Bread*, *Contemplative Link*, and *Antarctica Journal*, in which some of the poems first appeared.

Contents

Introduction

The title of this book of poems, *Watching the River Flow By*, alerts us that we are travelers and pilgrims in our lives on earth. We appeared here one day, and another day we will pass on. The earth is not our permanent home. On this trip of living, many things happen to us, good and bad, and we ask questions of what are our lives all about, looking for its meaning, wondering about the present and what the future will bring. We ask many questions, not always getting answers, and human life and its currents have a dimension of mystery that will always stay with us.

In my poems, I try to describe and celebrate those experiences in life that touch me and shed light and meaning on the trip I am taking. Nature has always been a rich experience for me, and my trips to the seashore, mountains, or sitting in my spring and summer garden prompt me to wonder about life and give me insights into the meaning of this journey on earth. My contact with nature and its beauty encourages me to meditate and contemplate and try to contact the divine, which is an important element in my pilgrimage on earth. The meditation movements that I am involved in give me encouragement and skills to grow in the contemplative path.

I make contemplative pilgrimages to shrines in Europe, Québec, and the United States and write poems about them. In these pilgrimages, I leave home and take a long trip to a holy place. At the shrines, there is time for meditation, silence, and religious activities. These trips are times of many graces, and I ask for help for my life and trip on earth. So in one sense, these pilgrimages are a symbol of my life on earth where I am a traveler on the way to my real home.

The 1960s had a profound effect on my growing up. I became aware of many social issues, such as the civil rights movement, anti-poverty movement, the peace movement, and so forth. That time made me sensitive to the problems of injustice, violence, and war that plague our existence. This influence of the 1960s has never left me, and I am still active in various movements dealing with these issues. My poems on social activism highlight the various activities, demonstrations, and marches in which I am involved and help me raise my voice and cry against the various injustices that are part of our world.

I have been lucky that the works of art that we have inherited through the centuries also are a source of wonder for me. They are beautiful and touch me. They also deal with issues of life and living and help me to wonder about and appreciate the things that pass around me. The beauty of art gives me encouragement to continue to march and keep going in the world, and my poems on art try to articulate this.

In conclusion, these poems are a testimony of my travels in life, and I have published this book hoping that readers will find some light and meaning in their pilgrimage on earth. Poets are people who see things and then write them down. We publish them so that other people might benefit and see more light and meaning where there is darkness. We are all in this boat together.

Seashore

Bench at Jones Beach

In loving memory of Margaret M. Ross-Adler from your family, friends, and colleagues. We love you and miss you more than the number of waves that roll down front.

Ordinary bench, wooden seat
with steel-iron frame gives it
strength. Wood a bit worn from all
the sun, wind, and saltwater.

Dedicated to Margaret Ross-Adler
by her family and friends. Bench looks over
sand into wide sea,
endless blue sky, cloudy days,
rainy days. At night looks at
black sky, stars, and constellations.

I wonder what secrets are whispered.
Secrets of living, dying, health,
sickness, peace, and war. Bench watches
endless stream of life
world universe.
I envy it—such a perfect
beautiful place to wander. Every day,
whole year, day and night.

I come to the sea,
want to touch mystery sky and seashore.
Let vastness wash and flow over me.

Bench—I on the same trip
travelling through the years with
its tears, laughter, health,
sickness, life and death. Bench sees it
all. We humans live it all.

Bench is persevering, just sits here,
does not give up. Example to me keep
walking in life, back and forth on
beach of life with sand, sky,
ocean water.

I should not become
overwhelmed, too distressed with
flow of life. Bench is here each day,
sunshine and rainy days. I have
to keep on walking through the
years, unraveling mysteries, finding
new ones.
Waves will not knock me down.

Quiet Seashore Day

Nerves on edge,
many things to do,
housework, poetry manuscripts,
concerns about my health.

Noise, violence of our world
never-ending wars.
Gaza and Charlie Hebdo,
harsh words, much hatred.

Feel my insides all upset,
looked forward to a day at
the sea. I was not disappointed.
Weather helped me.

Blue sky, cold wind
not too sharp. Jones
Beach pine trees soar
up, make no noise.

Dead yellow dune grass
gently swaying in the breeze.
They are awaiting the bugle of
springtime will be green again.

So life rolls on
New Year. What will
it bring? Hopefully good news—
only God knows.

I live in mystery. All of
us do, mystery of time,
mystery of God and Jesus,
invisible hands directing us.

Thank God I live near the seashore,
West End Beach.
I let it blow over me,
soothe me, strength for tomorrow!

Falling Waves

I see blue sea in the distance. Day is calm
but waves still come in.
They fall, pound on the surf,
whirlpool sand all upset. Foam all over the place,
water recedes, all begins over again.

Cycle, wildness, wet
touch me deep, echoes within me.
Life like the wildness of the sea,
endless waves and crashes.
I feel upheaval of the world.

I cry sometimes, tears down my face.
Why endless wars? So many
women and children killed.
Hatred, anger, I yearn for peace.
Where is it? Hard to find!

Waves of the sea, crashes,
enigma of life,
endless cycle.

I sit on the seashore,
look at vast sea sky.
I cannot grasp them—they are
beyond me. World is beyond
me!

Let me leave it to Jesus.
Despite it all, he had his
Easter Sunday.
Hopefully shares that with
us today.

Journey of My Life—Journey to God

Utter silence, blinding winter sun,
gentle breezes hardly noticeable,
surprising warmth for January
silent mystery!
In the distance pounding sea, waves crashing in, wild
repeating noise one right after the other.

Are these sounds of my life? Pounding?
Wildness? No control?
Mystery of pounding of the sea is the mystery of my life.
So many different currents, some dangerous,
others easy to swim in.

Utter silence of the day is utter silence of God
the beloved.
Crashing ocean cannot take away silence of the divine.
Stillness permeates all. It frames noise, and pounding sea
frames currents of my life.

How does it do it? Mystery?
Let me not ask too many questions!
Better let me feel the presence in silence,
presence of the beloved.

Like mysterious pounding of the sea,
my life pounds in mystery,
sometimes painful, other times with smiles.
Let mystery be dark and dim.
Presence of my beloved is there.

He will not leave me alone.
God hovers over all!

Winding Dune Road

Sand road, many footprints
wind into dunes, autumn
grass already brown, bushes losing
leaves. Here and there young pine trees
dark green against yellow-
brown vegetation.

Wind sharp,
inoffensive ocean breeze
comes on land, air fresh.
Road winds curves then straight,
heading for the sea.

I have been dreaming for a long
time to come here walk on
sandy road, feel its twisting turns
through the curves. Winding road
says something to me whispers.
I walk to uncover its secrets.

Road here all year long, day and night,
looking at sun, clouds,
stars at night. So lucky to be able to wonder, dream
in such beauty.

Not all is beauty now, brown dune grass
getting ready for winter, deep
sleep. Next year, spring's bugle
will blow, green will overcome brown, dry grass. New life
will come, cycle will begin again.

Such is life, has its cycles.
Road of life winds through dunes
of living and turns into the unknown.
Who can predict where it will go?
I cannot predict where my life will go.

There are many turns, dangerous
curves through the years. My life can
have much dry, brown dune grass, later
becomes green, big mystery
as the clear beach sky is
endless blue, no end, no limit.

I will keep on walking, my feet will
get tired in the sand. I will keep on.
Not give up!

Betsy Died at Jones Beach

Strange, I come to Jones
Beach for its beauty, ocean
water, peace and quiet.
Leave noise of city behind.

Strange, Betsy, a cousin
killed at Jones Beach.
Car slammed into her,
instantly killed.

She never wore a seat belt,
did not believe in them.
Was a policewoman,
perhaps felt above these things.

Husband wore a belt. Got
away with a leg injury.
Betsy, fifty-one years old,
always a friendly person.

Life is strange.
Beach place of beauty rest,
same beach place of
death accident.

I felt bad when I
heard the news, was
always friendly with me
although I did not see her often.

We live with contrasts,
conflicting things in life—they
tug at me. I feel it deeply,
part of the mystery of living.

God only knows the
answer to these things.
I have to live with mystery,
its darkness, the unknown.

I pray Jesus will give peace
to Betsy, such a quick
exit. She woke up at
the other end. We live by faith.

Life and Living

River of Life

We are all sitting here on
the shore, watching water move
past us. For the moment,
water is calm, reflecting lovely blue
sky. Other days, rough,
vast currents, strong, I would
not dare to swim. Would take me
out—that is it! Sometimes cannot
see dangerous currents hidden
underneath surface calm.

We all sit here enchanted by the
water. Such is life. So many currents
shifting, calm, dangerous can suck one in.

I do not understand the river, at times
have glimpses but flow is a big mystery.
Will continue to sit here alone or
with others, watching and wanting to
penetrate flow, currents.

I will take out my pad, write, words
will come, prying, probing
mystery, river, and its currents.

Someone asks me to read
what I wrote. I will—
words that point, open, explain,
bit of light in the mysterious river.

We are all in same boat,
boat of life. Does not seem
to be a rudder with oarsman.
Perhaps my words may find a
path, path through currents and water
as we continue our journey on
river of life.

Deeper-Down Things

I cannot tell you how many
books I have read, with my four
master's degrees and a doctorate. They
would fill many rooms.
I do not read that many
books anymore, such a change
for me. Why such a shift in my life?

Is reading a book too fast?
Am I missing something?
Paradoxically, I am still
busy in my life, but in another
way I am slowing down like
a boat coming to a dock.

I read more poetry now,
going through my library, reading poets
I have noticed through the years.

Boris Pasternak survived under
that tough communist Russian regime—
miracle. I listen to what he
says about life in those times,
price he paid to speak out.

Robert Frost writing about his life,
years in the mountains of Vermont,
New Hampshire meditating on what
passed around him.

Is this what I am doing now?
Watching the currents, passages
of life around me.
I am not looking for books to explain
more with their words, but
listening to poets with their imagery, symbols,
listening to my own feelings as I
continue my pilgrimage in this life,
pausing, watching, catching glimpses
of deeper down things.

Railroad Station Salamanca

I do not recognize it anymore.
I should not, is a new station,
not the old one of sixty years ago.

Despite this, many memories
are here. 1956, passed through
as a college student. I remember
visiting old and new cathedral.

1982, crisis in my life, visited
Salamanca, time of tears.

Memories lie here from the past,
now a modern station!
I do not know it, remember
only the old one.

Such is life, experience, hurts
loves, plans fulfilled, unfulfilled.
Life moves on. We move on. Jesus
extends his hands, pulls us through.

There is now a new railroad station.
My life is new also. Crisis, accidents
did not destroy me.
I fell. Jesus picked me up.

I continue on my new path,
living my years until the end,
like new railroad cars pulling
in-out of Salamanca's new station.

My Name

just now gold sandaled Dawn
—Sappho

Has someone called me? I believe so.
My breathing gives me a clue.
I feel at my center a presence there,
silent, dark, and unknowable.
Its mystery touches me.
Am immersed in darkness, light—
they mingle, weave the quilt of my life's journey.
I listen to the mystery, feel that
someone has called my name.
In the many currents, undertows of my life
I was remembered,
was not forgotten. Someone called me,
walked with me.

I feel, remember how I stumbled in my years,
hard streets with dangerous curves.
Was forced to walk, drive in the night.

But I hear my name. Voice calls me
from afar, not from this world
but from my center, coming from the mysterious presence,
giving my name a deep sound
different from the ordinary.
It now has an echo of depth,
meaning, cutting through all the confusion of life.

Someone calls my name, call of love,
special because it is from the divine, absolute.
I have a beloved who is totally different.
When he acts, he breaks all barriers.
I enter into a new world.

Darkness, mystery of my life still lay on me,
but I know—I have a beloved who calls, remembers me.

Mrs. Keller

Bright winter sunshine brightens house,
white siding seems so clear,
snow blanket adds to the light.
A face comes to mind—Mrs. Keller.
As a little boy I delivered meat to her door.
Worked for my father, local butcher.

House has changed,
years ago surrounded by a large porch,
country style.
Now all closed in, attic built out,
many new dormers peek out of roof,
extension to the back of house.
New immigrants rent out every corner,
money for the mortgage.
So many DirecTV dishes on the roof,
news from all over the world, from back home.

I sit in my car, protection from stiff winter wind.
Mrs. Keller is no longer here,
left everything behind, new owner emptied
out the place.
She lived there most of her adult life,
even cared for in the end years
loving son.

Mrs. Keller departed, radical break,
gone to a new life.
I do not know if she comes back sometimes
to see how different house is,
no more country-style wide porch.

Mrs. Keller's house reminds me
of my journey,
traveler on road of life.
Road has been long. My feet hurt.
Someday I will depart like Mrs. Keller.
My house will be sold, emptied out,
perhaps expanded to house new immigrants.

Road of life is a big mystery,
tells me house that I live in,
earth that I walk on
are not my final home.
I am on the way to my final home
destination.

Loving father ran out to embrace prodigal son
returning home.
Hopefully, loving father will run out for me.

Empty Store

Cold winter's day gray,
snow coming tonight.
Passed a closed, empty store,
windows covered with gates,
inside cleaned out,
painted white for new business.

Store empty, gone the business,
touch me, store is empty,
but memories are still alive,
will never go away.

My father bought butcher shop
from his uncle 1931.
Marriage followed shortly,
my mother the cashier.
Me—born a few years later in
apartment over store.
I came quickly, local doctor
ran over for delivery.

Young kid with my bike
delivered meat for my dad
all over the neighborhood.
Still see the faces.
No more busy butchers inside cutting,
packing meat, people waiting to be served.

While gazing at empty store,
elderly Greek lady passed looked also at
empty store, asked me what happened to the butchers?
Over forty years ago she moved into Jamaica Hill
neighborhood, only bought meat from my father,
brother, Leo and Leo. She misses them.
My father gave her nice lamb for the Greek Easter.

Strange! People, businesses, stores come, go,
store empty.
Neighboring bodega man says taxi service will open soon.
But memories are eternal, do not go away,
faces, voices, names, cuts of meat,
baloney, pot roast,
memories stay.
Life is a river, carries so much away,
but not memories. Like stones on shore
to hold on to, not everything is washed
away, give us strength to move
on, mystery of life.
Hopefully God is rudder of the boat
landing us on sandy, safe shore.

Winter Night

Night has come, winter night,
cold and dark, come early.
Streetlights show the way
for a few people walking.

Number of cars gets smaller.
Most people already home.
Local bus also empty,
few riders traveling late.

Darkness covers all.
Slowly silence grows.
People in their homes
leave streets empty.

New Year has begun,
time marches on,
year after year, season
after season.

Darkness of winter night,
sense of mystery, mystery of time,
of life,
mystery of God and Jesus.

Mystery of my life,
its ups and downs,
good times, bad ones,
smiles, laughter, tears, sobs.

Dwindling street activity,
darkness covering all
gives me time to calm
down and reflect.

I am busy but
take this quiet moment
to be in the presence of Jesus,
presence of the quiet.

Gives me a chance
to sort out, see
what is important?
Discard rubbish that accumulates.

Tomorrow sun will rise,
light returns, streets
get busy again. Hopefully
I will see my road, path better.

Silent Winter

Bitter cold and wind
touch the bones.
Snow coming and came,
same weather, no change.

I have to stay home,
not many activities,
outside meetings
cancelled—too cold.

Change for me, I have
time on my hands.
I am always busy,
many things to do.

Quiet descends on me,
vacant time. What
should I do? What can
I do?

Look at pictures of
beautiful art gives
me joy to see such
loveliness. My heart lifted.

Silence touches me.
Someone enters,
divine, the beloved,
space made for him.

I am now in
another way of living,
time, silence on
my hands, mystery.

I have to take advantage
of this moment, silence,
emptiness. Life is
not summed up in endless
running around.

Let me go deeper,
see different things.
I hear silent knock
at the door. Let me
open and savor it.

Cloudy, Damp July Fourth

Big holiday celebrations,
noise, fireworks,
cloudy day drizzling.
Few cars, no beach traffic.

Strange, silent day
for this July Fourth.
I am tired today,
long barbecue yesterday.

I feel the break, strangeness,
calm down inside.
Current of life flows
past me, fast so many things.

Have been busy all spring,
many things I had to do.
Felt the tiredness, takes
time for the strength to come back.

World makes me tired,
so many wars and hatred,
no end in sight.
I am caught in the whirlpool.

What to make of it?
No easy answers!
Pilgrimage to the Black
Madonna helped me.

Black Madonna sits in
mystery, is black
her son also. Do they
feel the whirlwind as I do?

Let me keep my eyes on
Black Madonna and child.
On this cloudy, quiet day
I have time to do it.

I do not know the answers
to everything, feel the quiet
is healing. Catch my breath
helps me keep rowing
in the boat of life.

Day after Eightieth Birthday

Party went well,
about thirty-five people.
Local Italian restaurant.
Food was good. People were happy.

Eighty years have
passed. Hard to believe.
I do not feel the
long time.

I should be happy
that I got this far.
I am still healthy,
can do my work, obligations.

I will see what the future
years will bring, happy days,
sad ones, laughter and tears.
Our lot on earth!

Let me keep my chin up.
I made it so far.
Hopefully I can make it
for what remains.

I have to keep my
confidence in Jesus, Good Shepherd.
Life is beyond me, all of us.
We are not in control.

Life is mysterious,
few answers, many questions.
I have to keep on walking.
Sure hand leads me on.

January 1, 2014

Calm day, winter cold, sunshine
this morning, later disappeared
behind high clouds. Streets are
quiet, people resting from
revelry last night. Old year gone,
new one arrived!

Dimness of
sun, quiet throw a shroud
of mystery on the day. Not much
activity, frenzy of the holidays.

Now time to think, rest,
look into mystery, time comes,
time goes! Like a flowing river
passes us by.

Where is it all
going? River already passed
many places, towns, cities,
still moving on its way to the sea,
ocean. Where is my life going?
Already passed many experiences, people,
joys, and tears.

River has deep, dangerous
undercurrents, can harm us. Life
same way, dangerous currents
brought tears to my eyes. Such is life!
We are not in control, things happen,
can hurt us.

But river, life keep flowing on.
I steer boat hoping to
avoid rocks. Am not always
successful. River is dark, mysterious
in its depth. So is life my life,
everyone's life. This will not
change, whole thing beyond me and all of us.
Some things are clear, can see them,
others dark. I will never understand.

I have to keep my head up, live
with light and darkness around me,
in me. This will not change
while I live here below.
What will happen afterward?
Good question!

Let me remember Jesus
loves me, boat of my life has
hit rocks and shoals in the river.
Jesus was always there. Boat
did not sink. Went on to different
waters.

Let me keep on steering.
Good Shepherd will bring me
to a safe landing.

Social Action

Climate-Change March 2014

What a crowd! I had not seen
so many people in the streets in
a long time, Occupy
movement resurrected.

Young people, old people, all colors,
nationalities, lots of noise, shouts,
slogans, speeches, music,
songs, musicians playing.

Central Park West jammed,
lines of people as far as the
eye could see. Balloons and signs
waving in the breeze.

Noise overhead, many helicopters.
Press? police? I hope the press
but fear police
watching us from on high.

I felt good with so many people,
long time in coming.
Movements grow, get knocked
down, have to lift themselves again.

Feet got sore, body was tired,
long day, march down Manhattan.
I felt a fire lit within me.
Hopefully this fire will touch
all of us, will be a long fight.

Banks

Lots of people on the street .
Saturday afternoon shopping,
warm summer day. Protestors
get together, signs, posters,
fliers, cardboard house
to put over our heads.

Protestors took off, walked
through crowded streets. People
looking, reading signs, flyers,
Citibank, Bank of America, HSBC,
you name them, busy making money
off the customers.

Marchers stopped at each bank
shouting, "Banks get bailed out.
We get shut out!"
Cardboard houses, painful
reminder of foreclosures.

People on the street, bank customers
looked, heard the shouts
of protest: "Banks corrupt,
doing people, houses, homes in."

People read flyers, asked
questions, learning painful
truth.
Protestors kept on marching
banks all over that neighborhood,
practically every corner.

Someone has to say something.
Things cannot just go on. Hopefully,
our feet will not get tired, our voices
dim. Road ahead long!
Let us stand together, keep on shouting.

May 1, 2012

Lots of people, electric crowd
signs galore, labor unions, students,
antiwar, anti-banks, immigrants,
you name it, they were there.

Musicians played, people sang
songs of protest, anger yearning
for peace, no more endless wars.
Pamphlets given out, news of
future protests.

Surprise! Occupy Queens sign drew people,
picture taking, asking what is
going on in Queens?

We started to march, long
line down Broadway the canyons.
Shouting, slogans, fighting words:
"Banks get bailed out.
We get sold out."

CUNY students vibrant
with their bullhorns, songs, shouts
demanding change. Reminded
me of my days at CUNY.

Air was electric, people's spirits lifted.
Springtime, sunshine, warm weather
gave us a boost, let us take to
the streets, shouting, let our
message come out. Spring means
rebirth. What is sleeping comes alive.

We marched to Wall Street
have to keep on marching, shouting,
singing. Walls of Babylon and money,
war-making have to
come down.

We dreamt of something new.
Let us march to Wall Street,
keep on marching.

Kill Anything that Moves *

"'Kill anything that moves."
These words kill me.
They echo back and forth in
my eardrums. They bang at
my heart, sounds of unbelief.

Things that I have known for many
years now come out in broad daylight. I wonder in
disbelief how can humans
be so cruel? Women, children massacred,
defenseless, they had no guns.

Long ago I lost belief in my country,
rhetoric of Washington.
We are an empire, conduct ourselves
as such. More and more wars,
corporations have more room,
make more money. I hear
these words, *democracy, freedom.*
What do these words mean to
all the massacred, innocent women and children?

I sit in my sorrow, drown within
it. What people do to one another?
What war pushes people to do?

We have to keep on marching, desperate!
Sore feet, blisters, long haul!
This trip will not end tomorrow.

I remember the words of Jesus:
"Blessed are the peacemakers
they shall inherit the earth."
He will give us the strength
to keep on marching. We cannot
live with what we have,
but march protest to build
what we dream of.

*Title of a book by Nick Turse on the atrocities committed by the
United States in the Vietnam War.

Dreams

Bright October Sunday, Indian summer,
clear, blue sky,
took subway to Church Street.
At post office, civil rights demonstration.
Martin Luther King was to come.
Excitement!

Good crowd but not too many people,
disappointment King did not show,
sent young disciple John Lewis,
charismatic man. Spoke with fire,
had us all mesmerized.

My eyes wide open, ears listening,
heart burning,
pangs for justice and pains of suffering.
America's blight, Black people,
poor people, not enough to eat, no work.

I never forgot that October afternoon
until today.
1960s dream time!
Young people, we were dreaming of a better world;
no need for lunch counter sit-ins,
voting marches to Selma..

Vietnam War, two to three million killed,
they wanted to be independent,
did not want the French, did not want us either!
It took thirteen years to stop the war,
many blisters on my feet.

Since then other issues came, still around.
Too many poor people need more jobs.
Already eight to nine years of war in Iraq and Afghanistan,
holocaust of the Palestinian people seems eternal,
sixty-two years.

But I can always look back.
October Sunday afternoon
1963.
Something was there, fire,
torch passed on.
I am glad it was passed on, did not
go out!
Pushes me to keep on marching, shouting
dreaming!
I am glad it was passed on, did not
go out! Pushes me to keep on marching, shouting
dreaming!

Zuccotti Square Revisited

May Day 2014

What a relief! Rains passed.
May Day afternoon sun
came out. I did not want to get
drenched again.

City Hall rally was good, labor groups
gathered by five for the speeches.
DC 37, 1199, Transportation workers, UTF,
adjunct teachers wanted equality, good pay.
Asbestos workers with their orange T-shirts,
LIUNA mostly immigrants. Only
work they can get dirty and dangerous.

Speeches were fiery, rousing crowd.
We need it, America low-
wage country. Good jobs sent overseas,
cheap labor exploited. Most Americans
do not feel effects of the recovery.

I walked down to Zuccotti Park, brought
back memories. Left a piece of myself in
that place. Time of dreams, action, speaking
out. Unforgettable!

I have memories. Tents, stalls of
Zuccotti Park no longer there. Dreams
never went away, justice, peace, equality.
They keep coming back push me to keep on
marching.

Sunny Day

I sat down, feet weary,
doing too many chores, warm sun
touched me. Amidst all, I felt quiet.
Clear sun highlighted the garden's colors—
greens, yellows, reds, fitting
in with quiet of sunshine.

Yet within me, I felt down, agitated,
not from the million chores I had to do.
Deep pain, I felt it
coming out of my breathing, my chest.
Had its roots in last Saturday
when thousands marched in Manhattan,
shouting, signs, banners against war.
Young, old, students, workers,
all together shouting for peace.
Fire of justice burnt in their hearts.

Despite rain, so many came determined.
At times, when showers were heavy,
marchers shouted louder.
Rain did not stop them.
I was there marching along.
Felt deep feelings within me,
heat from crowd touched me.
Tears came to my eyes, deep pain
from injustices of our world, violence and hate.

Quiet of the garden touches my shoulders,
alerting me that I cannot carry it alone,
being deluged with pain and suffering.
Sit in quiet, sunshine,
watch my breathing alerting me to
the presence of the beloved at my center, still point.

I am only a pilgrim on earth with weary feet,
cannot carry earth and its injustices.
My pain has me sit in darkness, where to go?
I know that God loves me, the world,
light in darkness, hope in pain.
Let me continue to sit in quiet, sunshine,
hand my pain to the Lord, my beloved.
Let him take it, giving me hope despite it all!

Thunder Clouds

Anti-Attack Iran Demonstration
Times Square, August 2, 2008

Clouds were moving fast, thick,
hanging low, noise of thunder,
signs imminent downpour.
Wind picked up, time to put on rain jackets,
open umbrellas.
It poured hard and steady.

I stood there, felt like taking a shower
in Times Square.
We looked at one another. Will rain
wash out our demonstration?
Are we strong enough to stand in water,
continue to shout?

Speakers spoke loud sheltered in a big truck,
words of imminent war, attack on Iran,
more fire in Middle East.
Do not tell me countless deaths of
mothers and children!

Rain downpour mingled with angry words.
Why such injustice in the world?
Noises of pounding rain,
noises of machine gun bullets!
Speakers continued, would
not stop.
Crowd did the same, soaking wet,
feet drenched, pants.
We stood firm, too much at stake!

On the next corner counter-demonstration.
American flags and Israeli flags,
demanding to send more troops.
That was harder to take than rain!
Sun never came out, rain continued
hard, pouring, then let up a bit.
We stood our ground.
We shall overcome!

Contemplation

Silence—Woods

Kilmarnock, Virginia

What a trip, hundreds of miles,
visiting a cousin, then poets' workshop.
Turning of the wheels still resonate
within me. At last, no more endless
driving, two days of peace, silence, meditation.

Quiet, stunning spot, water,
Chesapeake Bay. Air is still. Even
gentle breeze is silent. Rich green pine
trees like those of Cézanne,
stand at attention, do not move,
enchanted by the sunshine and silence.

Such is our lives, endless running around,
life in the big city. Many things to do,
hopefully good. Like the long trip,
one has to slow down stop!
Touch deeper-down things!

My life is not exhausted by these busy
activities, good as they may be.
In quiet, silence, woods,
a meeting mysterious,
human touching divine, two
lovers meeting, holding hands.

Strange, silent meeting stronger than
all the noisy activity in the world.
Sacred silence is where my real life is,
more real than running
around the big city. My beloved takes
my hand, will lead me through
ups and downs of city life helping me make
it a better place, lead the ship of
my life to a good, safe, final harbor.

For You Alone, My Soul Waits in Silence

Slowly, distinctly, I whisper,
"For you alone, my soul waits in silence!"

My voice rises from the depths,
words vibrate in my whole body,
coming from deepest parts of my center
whose depth is infinite,
endless tunnels, stairs, deep darkness,
so still noise never penetrates there.

I enter, descend slowly, but am hopelessly lost in mystery,
mystery of an encounter in my depths.
I meet my beloved, utter stillness.
My beloved speaks in silence,
clue to the divine's presence.

I repeat, "For you alone, my soul waits in silence!"
Feel resonance of the words,
words of love, longing, words of waiting.
I sit in utter silence. I feel nothingness,
but emptiness is full.
Out of darkness, out of mystery comes light.
What meeting could be more beautiful!

Sounds of Silence

I hear waves lapping shore in the distance,
deep sounds coming out of eternity.
Cool sea breeze touches my face,
silence coming from same eternity.
Endless blue sky says not a word,
hangs over all.

Sounds of waves wash deep within me,
open an abyss at my center.
My slow, quiet breathing points to it!
I feel a pain within my whole body,
pains of love, longing, and desire.
Abyss takes hold of me,
penetrates my whole self.
Abyss is mystery, darkness, and silence,
presence of my beloved.

My beloved is knocking at my heart, at my center.
Tears fill my eyes, but I can say no words.
I have no words to say!
Sounds of waves echo my endless longing.
Love, desire, feelings of fire close my throat.
My beloved is other, transcendent, beyond me
yet always deep within me,
presence I have, do not have.
Can only sit, wait, whisper:

"For you alone, my soul wants in silence."

Inner Emptiness

Harbor waters are still.
No strong wind is stirring. Calmness spreads
to the other shore, touches vast blue sky.
Sunlight is calm, not broken by fast-moving clouds.
No sharp gusts of winds strike my face.

Calmness ignites mystery, mystery of
a presence at my center.
I cannot grasp with my hands calmness
of sea nor of whole scene.
I cannot grasp mystery at my center.
I have no hands to do it, nor has anyone.
Utter darkness, utter infinity and stillness.
I shake my head, am lost in mystery,
mystery so close to me at my center but
also so far away.

Sadness touches me. My beloved
is here but not here. I have to live
with this distance. I feel its pain, loneliness.
Calm blue waters remind me of this.
I can feel beauty of the sea, but it slips through my hands.

Stillness, calmness remind me of my journey in life,
journey into mystery, mystery of ecstasy,
but also journey into darkness totally beyond.
I rest in this mystery stillness. Despite the otherness,
I feel a hand touching me,
guiding me into darkness.

Evening Hush

Gentle summer air comfortable
not hot, colors tone down,
sunshine has gone, hear
final chirps of birds in the trees.
Like a cat walking on freshly cut grass,
stillness descends on all,
no wind to disturb calm.
Was a long day, too many chores,
aching feet, e-mails, telephone calls,
decisions to be made.

Welcome relief to sit in quiet!
Let it roll over my whole body.
Deep sedative
calm takes me over. Even my
feet do not ache so much.
Look forward to this hour,
time for a visit.

Garden's hush opens up
an abyss at my center, still point.
Someone touches me, mystery, otherness.
No words are spoken, silence
the language of God.
Silence, calm, hushed garden
usher me into a presence,
presence of my beloved.
Let me rest in this quiet
visit, gift that puts a beautiful
end to a hectic day.
Someone is with me—that is all that matters!

Inward Journey

Summer day, warm, humid,
but not oppressive.
Clear sun brightens up,
yellow, blooming black-eyed Susans in the garden.
I sit in quiet, notice my heartbeat,
my breathing in and out
pointing to a presence within me,
my beloved.

Total mystery, otherness
that my quiet heart beats point to.
My beloved covers me,
embraces me. My whole body feels the touch.
I sit in mystery so deep within me.
I say nothing. I let
my breathing highlight the presence.

In the ebb and flow of my life,
in years gone by, in moments now,
in currents, undertows that almost
did me in,
someone was there, never let me go.
I bathe myself in this love.
Because of it I did not get lost
in crossroads, curves of the years gone by.
No dead-end streets,
always an exit!
How lucky I am—someone loves me!

Russian Orthodox Liturgy

I breathe deeply, in, out.
Smell of incense enters my nostrils.
Choir sings steadily in the
background, priest sings, choir
answers, much repetition.
Foreign language adds to mystery.

Incense rises to ceiling, passing golden
walls, icons. Incense burner's bells
clink softly.
Sunlight comes in the windows.
Hanging chandelier glows with
many lights. Assembly stands
quiet, periodically blessing themselves
with Russian cross. People walk around,
contemplate icons on walls. Tables
gently bow their heads to touch them.

Mystery hangs over all, penetrates
atmosphere, quiet, presence.
My continual slow breathing reminds me
divine within me at my center, still point.

Lord is present here amidst
golden icons, painted walls, repetitious singing.
Sweet-smelling incense covers
all in the church. One
need not speak—choir does that.

Mystery hangs over me. I enter into
another world, mysterious
liturgy hidden behind curtains.

I dare not say anything. What can
I say bathed in such mystery? Best
stand, kneel, bow with the assembly.
We know who is here, are awaiting
Lord's gentle touch, helping hand
for our pilgrimage here below.

On Pilgrimage

Pilgrimage

Castilla y León, Spain

Wide landscapes, endless wheat fields,
blazing sunshine, high mountains
topped with bonnets of snow,
medieval cities sitting on high hills,
massive walls giving protection!

John of the Cross wandered through these fields and flowers
looking to touch, meet his beloved.
I hear Teresa of Ávila pounding medieval streets,
crying out her message of reform,
falling in ecstasy over her beloved.

Images cross my mind of these holy places.
Fire begins to burn within my heart.
My feet feel hard, cobblestone, medieval streets.
Images of mountains, fields touch me.
I feel a presence at my center.
It moved John of the Cross wandering in the same fields.

Presence overwhelms me.
I am covered with an invisible shroud
touching my innermost heart.
I continue to walk through medieval streets,
wander in wheat fields, feel
snow-capped mountains,
steep walls, fortresses overwhelm me.
They all introduce me, lead me into silence,
quiet, stillness, and mystery.

John and Teresa bring me into the labyrinth of my center.
No words can reach it.
I cannot speak!
I sit in darkness,
my insides burning.

I remember words of John of the Cross:
"In a dark night
burning with fires of love!"

Saint Anne of Beaupré

Québec

Quiet day, not much
sunshine.
Later after one thirty, sun
burnt fog away.

I sit on a hill
overlooking the basilica,
vast vista over
wide Saint Lawrence River.

Vast and deep,
ocean boats can travel
on it. They glide slowly
along the horizon.

Saint Anne picked
beautiful spot for her
basilica. Pilgrims
love to come here.

Through the centuries,
Saint Anne draws travelers.
Christians recall her goodness.
She listens to their petitions and cares.

Could not have put
basilica on a better spot,
vast Saint Lawrence,
vast love of Saint Anne for us.

As the river winds
down to the Atlantic,
it gets wider and bigger.

So too in our lives,
we have many cares,
some heavy, others light,
not even to mention
heavy load of our world.

Like the flowing river,
Saint Anne is there
walking with us.
Someday we will reach
ocean of eternal life.

Silence of Mary

Mary, Queen of the Heavens
Montréal

Simple chapel,
simple church,
silence of the chapel
touches me.

Mary does not say
anything. Lets
us know she is
there, silent and listening.

I came a long way to
make this trip, pilgrimage.
Ride long and tiring.
I made it.

I want to thank Mary
for being here. She knows
all my problems,
problems of the world.

Silence is here,
language of God.
Mary learned it,
covers me with it.

I sit in the chapel,
a pilgrim who travelled
long distance to touch
the divine, the beloved.

Mary assures me
trip was not in vain.
Jesus, Mary are
listening, touch me with silence.

Marie-Rose Ferron: Stigmatic

Woonsocket, Massachusetts

Sunday morning, quiet reigns
over cemetery grave of
Marie-Rose Ferron.
Silence that haunts,
full of mystery and presence.

Silence is not empty,
touches me
at my center, still point.
Quiet watches over me as
gentle, cool morning breeze.

Silence is full, presence of the
divine, the beloved,
full of presence of Marie-Rose,
full of mystery of life,
death, wars, violence, and injustices.
Marie-Rose's wounds bleed from these.

I sit in silence
letting mystery's touch overwhelm me.
It overwhelmed Marie-Rose.
Her wounds bled from it.

Such is our journey in life.
We carry a heavy load, our sins,
sins of the world.

I made a pilgrimage
to the grave of Marie-Rose.
Will never understand life, its dark side.
Marie-Rose did not either.
She carried that burden.
Wounds show it.
She will give me strength,
carry burden of living.

Tombstone

Marie de l'Incarnation
Québec

Stark, black tombstone,
heavy, large,
Marie de l'Incarnation
1599–1672.

Black sets tone for the room,
silence, depth, and mystery.
Tombstone, large, heavy,
adds to the mystery.

I hear the words of John
of the Cross in his famous poem
"In a Dark Night."
Darkness and blackness,
mystery and depth.

Poem filled with passion.
Two lovers meet in the dark
night,
filled with life and light.

Marie's tombstone, black,
dark, filled
with love and life.
Her lover, Jesus, she called
him her bridegroom.

I sit in the presence of such
dark, black passion, love.
I ask Marie to help me
enter and feel the love,
unity between them.

Life is mysterious.
So is love. Marie
fell in love with the divine
despite the night and darkness.

We cannot expect much more on earth.
John's poem and Marie's tombstone
tell us this.
I am in a dark night,
hope to feel the pulse of this love.

Black Madonna

Altoetting, Germany

Dark chapel pierced by candlelight.
Silver and gold glittering!
Stately candles on the altar
add solemnity. Many yellow
roses blend with gold and silver.

In the middle, small, dark
statue woman with a child
dressed in black, gold,
holding a golden rose.

Silence reigns in the chapel.
Many people pilgrims,
no talking, stand at attention
in presence of the Black Madonna.

Statues centuries old,
a thousand years, who knows?
People travel, come from far,
wide like me.

We carry our human load,
ourselves and our world.
Many clouds of thunder
need more rays of sunshine.

Myself with all the
crowd stand here
in silence. No spoken
words, deeper ones inside of us.

Dark skin of the virgin,
child mysterious,
gives us hope in the
road of life, our earthly voyage.

I know that the virgin
with child is listening.
We all stand in silence
praying and hoping.
It will all work out.

Railroad Station

Einsiedeln, Switzerland

Trains arriving, departing,
in, out! Pilgrims come,
go to a holy place,
want to visit the Black Madonna.

Such is life, comings, goings
like the trains, things,
experiences come, go.
Where will it all end up?

I sit in the waiting room,
watch the train movement.
I am a pilgrim en route
visiting the Black Madonna.

Over the years, millions
came here asking, petitioning,
brought their burdens to
their heavenly mother.

I am doing the same,
carrying my burdens,
burden of the world
around me.

It is raining today,
quite cold, snowing on the
mountaintops.

Let me not be discouraged
by the weather. It rained
through the centuries on the pilgrims,
on the trains.

I need faith that cuts
through the fog, cold,
rain. Pilgrims before me
did it. Trains do it.
Now it is my turn.

Haiki and
Setsuwa Poetry

Haiku

March earth, dark, cold, damp.
Surprise! Yellow crocus smiles,
greets me. Spring has come.
***

Bright spring sun bathes all,
knocks at slumbering garden.
Soon lilacs, roses.
***

Dark-blue hyacinth,
mysterious, elegant,
deep soundings touch me!
***

Walking in the garden.
Shock! Fire! No! Forsythia,
yellow explosion!
***

Morning Glory

Hi! Morning glory,
pink, bright-eyed, so many
throw me sweet kisses!
***

Helen Hayes

Helen Hayes, yellow,
pink, soft rose, so elegant.
I fall in love.
***

Lilies of the Valley

Misty, cool, dark, deep
day, early spring. Sweet fragrance!
Perfume touches me.

Setsuwa Poetry

Spring Chores

I was busy legs, arms flying
pushing machine
sweat grass weeds cut.
Wait! Red azaleas kiss me.
***

My Little Kids

I laugh, box of wild firecrackers,
red, pink, yellow,
purple, orange, white
portulacas show-offs.
***

Blue Monday

I feel heavy, down.
Portulacas
laugh, smile, yellow,
pink, red tell me wake up! Smile! Laugh!

Art

Artists of the East End

I love Long Island,
surrounded by water,
ocean waves rough, calm seas too!
Miles of clean sand, soft on feet,
washed by never-ending waves,
blue sky, cloudy sky, endless variety,
bright sunshine, dim, cloudy, rainy days.

Rough winds coming off ocean,
brushing my face, chilling body,
endless colors, sun, clouds
play with one another, constantly changing
light and shadows.

Artist of the East End drawn to
shore, sands, sunlight of Long Island.
Paintings splashed with colors rich, thick,
bright yellow, red, orange jump on page.
Darker blue, brown, black,
more somber mood, rainy day.
Lines are sharp like boundaries
between sand and water.

For generations, artists came to East
End, walked sands enraptured by
sunshine, breathing in brisk sea air,
endless changing colors and space.

Ever-changing sea, sand, shore triggered
their genius, had to put the scenes on
canvas, made them happy, moments of
ecstasy, colors and shapes.
Now they pass it on to me!

Russian Icon

Our Lady of Vladimir

Soft touch, gentle head
bows, touches baby's face.
Mother's eyes deeply mysterious
looking into eternity.

Baby looking up, holding on to mom.
Mother's head covered with black shawl,
dropping down golden background
light from heaven shot through with divinity!

I am touched, feel quiet beauty
wrapping around me,
washing me in mystery,
touches of the divine,
the beloved!

Mother's eyes reach me,
include me in her meditation.
Wants me to stay quiet,
not run away.
Mother loves me too, taking me
by the hand, leads me to her son.

I feel delirious ecstasy in my eyes.
Mystery overwhelms me. Radiance
of Russian icon tells me,
"You are loved! Do not worry!"

Mystery of the mother is beyond
me, but her eyes watch me,
holding me, taking me by the hand
until my journey ends.

Winged Victory

La Victoire de Samothrace

It was so many years ago. Student
in Paris visited the Louvre.
Entered door, climbed marble
staircase, lightning, beauty strike me.
A statue!

Vibrant, moving, thrust
into action, winged victory.
Its age? Thousands of years
have not fatigued its force.

I stood in wonder, stand in
wonder still today, captivated
by its stunning energy, poster on
wall repeats original dazzle in my eyes.

Have lived with poster
for so many years.
They say things of beauty are everlasting.
Could be true! Statue may
disappear, poster too.
Can still feel
its lightning, beauty touching, captivating me.

Vietnamese Madonna and Child

Finely chiseled, delicate, slim faces,
Asian eyes, unfolding robes
red, black.
Madonna's head tipped toward baby.
Child nestled on mother's body.

Whole picture silent, so quiet .
Golden halo around head,
aura of divinity.
I rest in peace, quiet of picture,
feel it touch me, vibrations within
my heart.

I cannot forget, still see pictures French army.
My country waged war there so many years,
1940s, 1950s, 1960s. We wanted
to keep the people down, killed millions,
uncountable victims,
massacres, whole villages,
only God knows total dead.

Vietnamese Madonna, child, pictures of war,
clash, such is life! Why war?
Mystery!
Who knows the answer? I do not!

Madonna and child's picture exude mystery, beauty.
War machines are gone, planes,
napalm, quiet picture remains.

Someone gave it to me in 1955.
I never threw it out.
Too beautiful, haunts me.
I rest in this beauty,
giving me hope, so many wars in the
world until today.

I have to keep the faith!
God is present, acting in touching picture
of Vietnamese Madonna and child.
I never threw it out.

Hilltop at High Noon

Expressionist Landscape

Feel myself being taken up,
up into sunshine, light, soaring
clouds, imposing mountaintops,
rich green baked by sunshine.
Trees stand at attention, branches
thick with green leaves reaching up
knowing golden light is their
lifeline.

Clouds, trees, sunshine, mountains are
happy, bursting with life,
ecstatic in their beauty.
Ecstasy touches me, feel it brushing
my face. My insides are burning.
Am floating in thin air, mountains,
sunlight. Am touching another
world resting in its beauty. Joy!

Charles Burchfield
Hilltop at High Noon
1925

Adam

Tilman Riemenschneider, sculptor

Finely chiseled face, mouth, curly hair,
dreaming, gazing, questioning.
Adam dazzled look, asking
I am here, but where am I going?
Standing next to Eve, his companion,
another mystery.

Adam began his journey on earth
in life, mountaintops.
He walked, tripped, picked
himself up. Never lost that
dazzled look, life amazed him,
kept dazzled look he had
at creation.

He asked questions. Not many answers
were forthcoming, some helpful, others
not. Such is life!
Life is dazzling, so many
events, boat on rough seas.

My life the same,
have to remember someone put me
here just like Adam.
He looked dazzled, trip
of life is beyond us. We are not
in control. We know the Lord loves
us, will not let our hands go.
So we look dazzled like Adam
walking into mystery, holding on to
a hand, hand of God.

Maria

San Ildefonso Pueblo, New Mexico

Black pottery elegant as
Princess Diana, still,
rounded shape points to deep mystery.
Maria the artist was famous,
rediscovered art of pottery making
sadly forgotten by Indians in the conquest.

Pottery sits on dining room table,
exudes beauty like perfume.
Blackness catches my eye.
Black has nothing but still beautiful.
Held me for countless years.
Bought it in 1950s
traveling in Indian country.

I never stop looking at it.
Shape, silence, black
lead me into another world
far from tumult of today.
Wars and violence get me down.
I shake my head at such bloodshed.

Blackness, stillness of Maria's
pottery gives me glimpses of another world.
Hopefully it will win out in the end.

Our Lady of Fifth Avenue

Black Madonna
Saint Thomas Church

One does not have to travel far.
Make a pilgrimage to Lourdes or Fatima.
Right here in the heart of Manhattan
stately statue, Mary with child,
aura of holiness, sacred
black bronze.
Mary and child gaze into mystery,
eternity.

Darkness of face, figures, clothing
draw us.
Statue exudes deep silence
reaching into silence of God.

Blackness has nothing.
Here has everything,
leading us to walk into eternity,
into dark mystery of God.

Mary with child,
take us by the hand,
hand of love.

In utter blackness and mystery
someone calls our name,
our beloved,
call of love,

an encounter,
one that is eternal,
one that is faithful.

Call beyond human ones
that come, go,
call that grasps us, shapes us,
gives us peace the world cannot give.

Black Madonna, child sit in mystery,
inviting us to fullness
that no words can explain.

Adirondack Mountains

NEW YORK

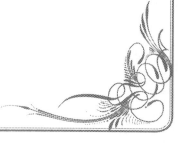

Adirondack Pines

Stately pines reaching to sky,
deep blue that only
Adirondack Mountains can paint.
Sun is clear, strong.
Tree branches reach out for its
life-giving nourishment.

Pines, sky, sunlight,
each a silence
broken only by gentle breeze
whistling through pine trees.
Breeze, so peaceful, so soft, adds to
silence of the woods.

So many years I walked, sat
among these stately pines.
Why do I come back?
I tell my friends I meet someone here.

Silence of Adirondack pines
echoes silence of God, absolute,
my beloved.
Being there is a walk in mystery,
mystery in the Adirondack blue sky,
also a presence
within me at my center, my still point.

I rest in this mystery letting gentle breeze
touch me,
soft kiss of someone who loves me.
Feel my breathing in and out pointing to
presence at my center.

Continue to look at blue sky, soaring pines.
Let silence, beauty run over me,
inundate me, embrace me.
Say no words because in silence of pines
my beloved is wooing me.

Gentle call!
No words of mine fit the situation
I sit in quiet, let it wash over me.
Joy!

Footsteps

How many years have I come to these
mountains? So many years!
My whole life and more!
Come here looking for someone,
for traces in winding paths,
forest, silent Adirondack pine trees
in sunlight playing back and forth trying to get through
the leaves, silence of giant boulders,
brown, dark earth covered with
autumn's leaves.

My life is like Adirondack trails,
up and down, level then precipitous,
blind curves going up to endless heights.
Through the endless turns of my life,
I have come to the mountains.

A presence called me, touched me,
wooing me to love the absolute, the divine,
even alerting me to upcoming disasters.

Despite harshness of the mountains
trails, ruggedness of
twists and turns of my life,
quiet softness of the presence, call of
love, call wooing me was stronger
than rough trails.

Beauty of the mountains won over their harshness.
Reminds me that the call of love from my beloved
wooing me won over the wounds,
dead-end streets of my life.

Now I know why I come back to the mountains
each year.
In their blinding beauty, I am looking for
someone, desire, desirous for a touch.
Let me feel happy, confident I am
still on this trail, straining for
spotting footsteps,
traces of the divine.

Come and Go

To end my two-week pilgrimage
to Québec, I stopped for a night
in Lake Placid in the
Adirondack Mountains.

Arrived at the hostel.
It was a quiet evening.
Clouds coming in,
rain tonight.

I breathed the
Adirondack air, so
different from the city air,
clear, fresh, smell of pines.

Memories came back to me.
I hiked, backpacked for fifty
years.
I fell in love with the
mountains.

I have vivid memories
of the mountains, views,
smell of pine trees, different
people I met. Still feel the body sweat
on steep climbs.

I do not climb anymore.
Hard decision, it was time.
My body is just human,
cannot push it too hard.

Mountains, my climbing
came and went.
Such is life.
Through the years, people,
experiences, tears, laughter
came and went.

How to make sense of it all?
How to remember it?
That is why I make
pilgrimages.

In the ebb, flow of the years,
pilgrimage shrines are
still here. They lead me
to a world that does not pass away.
I meet a world, presence
who loves and cares for me,
cares for the world, crazy
as it is.

This gives me hope, people, things
of life come, go.
I see a light, never goes out,
leading me on in the seeming darkness.

Christmas

Christmas Tree

Heavy snow outside.
World covered in white.
Muscles ache, shoveling, paths
needed to be cleaned.

Wind and ice outside,
inside lighted Christmas tree, island of peace,
no wind to blow it over,
stands straight with red, green,
blue lights, some twinkling,
light bounces off colored balls.

My eyes drop, see crèche beneath tree,
peaceful, surrounded by snow.
Crèche exudes a silence, peace,
a few sheep, poor shepherds,
Mary, Joseph, the babe,
poverty exudes its own silence!

Whirling wind, snow outside,
are they not the world?
Problems swirl around us.
People feel they are drowning in crises
encroaching on every side,
Wall Street crashes and scandals,
endless wars, countless innocent deaths,
lame-duck president babbles on.

Let me look again at crèche,
little babe.
My insides burst, pangs of hope.
I am a poor pilgrim on earth,
weary feet, tattered clothes.
Little babe brings me hope, brings all mankind hope!

No words of mine can express this
light at end of tunnel!
I sit in quiet tone of Christmas tree,
let it roll over, bathe me.
I breathe quietly and evenly
adding to peace,
peace and hope to hold me in New Year!

Christmas Eve Vespers

Wintry day, low, heavy
clouds pour rain down on the city.
Winds are sharp at times.
Luckily rain washes away snow, sloppy ice.
Heaviness hangs over all.

I feel it is not whole story.
Tomorrow is someone's birthday.
Light shines in the night.

Darkness touches our world—
Wall Street collapse, scandals, unemployment,
endless wars, more to come.

Eagerly, I look for light
Christmas vespers, boys' and men's choirs,
powerful organ, incense,
song, music wash over me.
I feel limp, grasp out for
hope the birthday brings.

My heart beats, chest is tight,
tears fill my eyes
tears that await hope to dry them.
Music, voices give me a glimpse of
another world. Jesus is born
not to leave us alone.
Despite it all, warm hands embrace us.

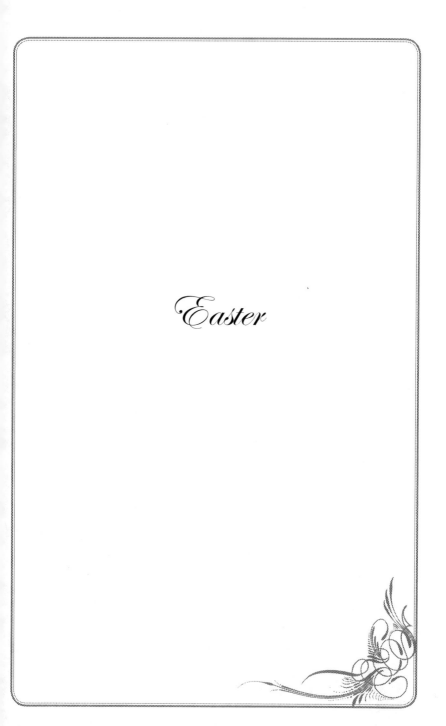

Easter

Sunshine—Easter Morning

Bright, clear sunshine, early
Easter morning, lovely
blue sky, hardly a cloud.
Sun brightens spring garden,
smiling yellow daffodils, mysterious
blue, pink, and white hyacinths.

Aroma touches you a mile away.
Pink, yellow primrose,
small but not the least.
Gentle breeze, daffodils shake
their heads in joy.
Sunshine covers all. Colors
blend together like a concert.

I am happy in the sunlight.
Light is celebrating
the risen Lord.

Jesus's life, death, and resurrection
overwhelm me. Such a good man
caught in the web of evil intentions.
Such a good man! Why such an end?

Jesus's passion repeated many times in
suffering of good people,
innocent but devastated,
endless wars, violence, hatred.

Sunlight is quiet. Strong, clear
overcame darkness of the night.
Light, day, night, darkness,
big mystery.

Life has many turns.
Clear sunshine gives me hope.
Lovely and beautiful,
giving a good ending to a sad story,
our story too!
The Father wanted a happy ending
despite it all!

Printed in the United States
By Bookmasters

"Bob Trabold's poetry is reflective of the rich life he lives. His work powerfully
gently centers on the spiritual core and peaceful aspects of human existence. His poe
are thought-provoking, insightful and most of all inspiring." Tone Bellizzi, Direct
Davault Artists' Café

"Robert Trabold masterful style of his long-awaited collection '*Watching the River Fl
By: Selected Poems*'…with a poetic voice …blends with that of the Endless River. W
liquid poems, meditation, haikus, spirituality travel through the landscape of Euro
translating artifacts of words bringing that verse back into the 21st century."

"…Drifting back to the days of his youth, standing up for civil rights anti-war and nuk
the environment and other social injustices – his poetic eye comes full circle back
the road to the shore of the ancient river returning back to the ocean of time and t
cosmic journey." James Romano, Performance Poets Assoc. of Long Island

Robert Trabold, Ph.D. lives in New York City, has a vari
academic background, speaks 5-6 languages and has do
much work on social and religious issues with people a
immigrants in urban America. He writes various kinds
poetry and some have been published in Soul Founta
Newsletter Marie de l'Incarnation, Newsletter Ther
Neumann, Antarctica Journal, Ravens Bread, Contemplat
Link and on HYPERLINK "http://www.contemplativepath.co
www.contemplativepath.com. He has a blog www.bobtrabold.co
and each month posts a contemplative poem with an article
meditation, silence, pilgrimages, etc.

He is a social activist and participates in various movements to promote more peace a
justice in the world.

U.S. $11.99

ISBN 978-1-5043-6269

511

9 781504 362696

b

BALBOA.
PRESS

A DIVISION OF HAY HOUSE